# LEAN JOHN
## CALIFORNIA'S HORSEBACK HERO

# LEAN JOHN
## CALIFORNIA'S HORSEBACK HERO

### Randall A. Reinstedt

*Illustrated by Ed Greco*

*Ghost Town Publications*
*Carmel, California*

Randall A. Reinstedt's
**History & Happenings of California Series**
Ghost Town Publications
P.O. Drawer 5998
Carmel, CA 93921

Manufactured in the United States of America

10  9  8  7  6  5  4  3  2

Library of Congress Catalog Number 96-75248
ISBN 0-933818-26-2 Hardcover
ISBN 0-933818-81-5 Softcover

Edited by John Bergez
Cover design and illustrations by Ed Greco
Interior design and typesetting by Erick and Mary Ann Reinstedt

*This book is dedicated to Lean John, and to all of California's other unsung heros*

# LEAN JOHN'S RIDE

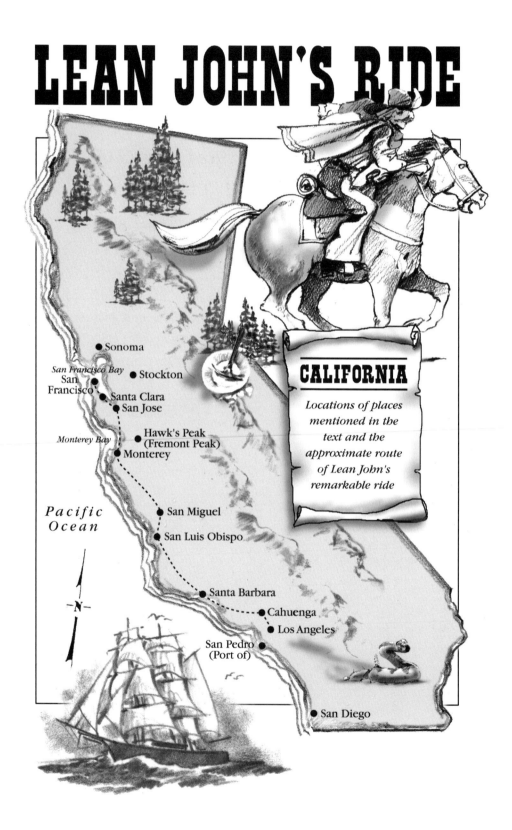

Sonoma

*San Francisco Bay*
San
Francisco

Stockton

Santa Clara
San Jose

*Monterey Bay*

Hawk's Peak
(Fremont Peak)
Monterey

**CALIFORNIA**

*Locations of places
mentioned in the
text and the
approximate route
of Lean John's
remarkable ride*

*Pacific
Ocean*

San Miguel

San Luis Obispo

Santa Barbara

Cahuenga

Los Angeles

San Pedro
(Port of)

—N—

San Diego

# *Introduction*

The history of California is one of the most colorful of any state, and one of the most exciting times of all was the decade of the 1840s. During that short ten-year period, the flags of Mexico, the California Bear Republic, and the United States all were raised over parts of California. For a while, powerful England also cast its eyes on the future Golden State. If things had turned out a bit differently, today you might be a citizen of Mexico, England, or even an independent country!

Of course, you know that in the end it was the Stars and Stripes that flew over California. But before that could happen, some areas of the future state changed hands several times. Many brave men fought to defend "their" country, including both Americans (citizens of the United States) and *Californios* (Spanish-speaking citizens of Mexican California). Some of those long-ago fighters are remembered today as true California heros.

This book is about one of those heros, a man by the name of John Brown. His Spanish-speaking friends called him Juan Flaco, which means "Lean (Thin) John," and he is remembered best as Lean John to this day. I think of him as California's own horseback hero.

I'm sure you've heard of a number of "horseback heros" who made famous rides or accomplished other feats. The best-known to Americans is probably the Revolutionary War hero Paul Revere. A silversmith in Boston, Massachusetts, Revere galloped through the night to warn the Minute Men that a force of British soldiers was on its way to the town of Lexington. (The Minute Men were armed volunteers who prided themselves on being ready to fight "at a minute's notice.")

Revere's "midnight ride" became one of the best-loved tales of the American Revolution, in part because of a poem that was written by Henry Wadsworth Longfellow in 1861. Thanks to Longfellow's poem ("Paul Revere's Ride"), generations of American children have played at imitating the great patriot, riding make-believe mounts and shouting "The British are coming! The British are coming!"

Many people today don't remember that Revere's ride was only partly successful. He did succeed in arousing the Minute Men, but he was captured by the British after leaving Lexington for Concord, about five miles away. (His two companions, Willam Dawes and Dr. Samuel Prescott, managed to elude capture. However, only Prescott made it to Concord.)

Interestingly, another American patriot made an even more impressive nighttime journey about a week later. Unlike Paul Revere, 16-year-old Sybil Ludington is little remembered today. Yet this young woman also made a horseback ride in the dark of night to warn American rebels about a British attack. In fact, the adventurous Sybil rode more than twice as far as Paul Revere—and she completed her journey successfully besides! Because of her daring ride, American patriots gathered from far and near to battle the British at Danbury, Connecticut, in April, 1777.

There have been many other horseback heros in American history. Like Paul Revere, Sybil Ludington, and John Brown, many of them performed their deeds during times of war. Others gained their fame in peacetime. You may have heard of the riders of the Pony Express, who braved the American frontier to carry mail on horseback. Working in relays, these fearless and talented riders covered a distance of nearly 2,000 miles from St. Joseph, Missouri, to San Francisco. The Pony Express was in operation for only about a year and a half (from April, 1860, to October, 1861), but the exploits of the "pony boys" are still remembered today.

These heros of yesteryear all showed great skill and daring. Certainly many more brave men and women have achieved great feats as horseback riders. Yet it's safe to say that none of them was more courageous or talented than the man you will read about in this book.

Like Sybil Ludington, Lean John doesn't have a famous poem in his honor and is remembered today mostly by history buffs. And like Paul Revere, some might say that he didn't quite achieve all that he set out to do. Does either of these things make him any less of a hero? Listen to his story, and decide for yourself.

# Lean John
# California's Horseback Hero

## A Terrible Mistake

To appreciate the tale of Lean John, we must travel back in time to the 1840s. As I mentioned in the Introduction, this decade was an exciting period in the history of the future Golden State. It was also a confusing time when no one could foresee which country would end up controlling California.

When the 1840s began, California was a part of Mexico. (Mexico had gained its independence from Spain about 20 years before.) But more and more pioneers from the United States were coming west, and many of them ended up in California. Meanwhile, England controlled the territory to the north, including much of the present-day states of Oregon and Washington. In the eyes of many British and American adventurers, Mexican California was a prize just waiting to be claimed. (Because England is a part of Great Britain, people from that country may be called either "English" or "British.")

In 1842, an event happened that showed just how confusing things could get. Believing that war with Mexico had begun, an American naval force seized Monterey, the capital of Alta (Upper) California under both Spanish and Mexican rule. For the first time, the American flag flew over California.

A few hours later, the conquerors of Monterey learned that they had made a terrible mistake. The United States and Mexico weren't at war after all! With embarrassed apologies, the Americans lowered their flag and returned control of the city to Mexico.

How could such a mistake happen? To answer this question, we need to imagine how things looked to the commander of the United States naval force in the Pacific, Commodore Thomas ap Catesby Jones.

As the 1840s approached, trouble was brewing between the neighboring countries of the United States and Mexico. For years, Americans had been pushing south and west into Mexican lands. In 1835, Americans in Texas joined in a revolt against Mexico and established their own independent republic. Many people in the United States looked forward to making Texas a state. Others had their eyes on still more Mexican territory. Some people were talking openly of war with Mexico.

Meanwhile, the American government was worried that the British might try to take California for themselves. With these things in mind, Commodore Jones was given orders to seize certain California ports if war broke out—and to make sure he got there before the British!

Early in September of 1842, Jones's fleet was anchored in the South American harbor of Callao, Peru. Jones was keeping a watchful eye on a small fleet of English warships. Suddenly, three of the British ships hoisted anchor and sailed from the harbor. Apparently, orders from England had reached the fleet's commander,

British Rear Admiral Richard Thomas. But where were the English warships (called "men-of-war") headed?

At about the same time, Jones received a report causing him to think that the United States and Mexico had gone to war. There was also talk that Mexico might let the British have California to keep it out of American hands. Naturally, Jones thought that Admiral Thomas had received similar information and was on his way to California.

The commodore had no way of checking with his superiors in Washington, D.C. In those days, it would have taken weeks for a message to travel back and forth. By that time, California might be lost for good!

With the English already on their way, the American commander did the only thing he could. Barking orders to his men, he prepared to set sail for Monterey!

# Beat the British!

Commodore Jones's flagship, the *United States*, together with a smaller ship, the *Cyane*, made a straight run for California's capital community, more than 3,000 miles away. Thinking he was in a race with Admiral Thomas, Jones spared neither man nor ship in his effort to beat the British to Monterey.

On October 19, 1842, the *United States* rounded the Monterey Peninsula's Point Pinos (Point of Pines). Anxiously scanning the harbor, Jones was relieved to see that there were no English warships in Monterey Bay.

With the British nowhere in sight, the commodore proceeded to capture a Mexican vessel that was making its way out of the bay. Together with the captured Mexican craft, the two American men-of-war cautiously entered the harbor. With the Stars and Stripes flying, the tiny fleet dropped anchor close to El Castillo, a small fort that overlooked the water.

Lying at anchor in the harbor was an American craft, the *Fama*. This ship had recently arrived from the Hawaiian Islands. One of its officers told Jones that rumors of war had reached the Islands. In fact, the officer had heard talk that the English were going to take control of California.

These reports added to Jones's worry that Admiral Thomas's warships might sail into the bay at any moment. Meanwhile, the Montereyans on shore looked as if they were preparing to defend the capital. Jones also noticed that no Americans came from the town to greet him. Considering all these things, the commodore decided to take action.

At 4 p.m. Jones sent a messenger to shore under a flag of truce. The messenger carried a note that was taken to Juan Bautista Alvarado, a former governor of California and a leading citizen of Monterey. Contained in the note was a stern demand: Surrender the capital at once to the United States of America!

Alvarado might well have been puzzled by the Americans' demand. Was the United States really about to seize California? Had war broken out? If so, no one had told him!

After receiving the note, Alvarado huddled with the local military commander as well as other officials and citizens. Soon they reached a decision. Monterey would surrender without a fight!

At 11 o'clock the next morning, Commodore Jones sent 150 marines and sailors to the Monterey shore. Meanwhile, the Mexican troops paraded out of the fort with colors flying and music playing. Straight to the

government house they marched, where they solemnly gave up their weapons.

A few hours later, Commodore Jones was studying papers that were found in the office of a Mexican official. The papers contained information that was more recent than the report Jones had received in Peru. As he read them, it dawned on him that the United States and Mexico were not at war after all!

Upon realizing his mistake, Jones promptly ordered his men back to the ships. As the red-faced Americans sailed away, the local *Californios* breathed a sigh of relief. Little did they know that this strange episode actually foretold the future. In a few short years another naval force would raise the Stars and Stripes over their capital community—this time for keeps!

## Hawk's Peak and the Bear Flag Revolt

After Commodore Jones left Monterey, the Mexican flag once again flew peacefully over California. But the Mexican authorities still had reason to be nervous about the United States, and about the Americans who were already living in California.

Although California was at peace, leaders in Washington, D.C., continued to talk of gaining more land for their booming country. Then, in 1845, the United States Congress voted to annex Texas (that is, to make this vast region officially part of the United States). As tensions continued to build, the threat of war hung like a dark thundercloud over Mexico and its ambitious neighbor to the north. Once again, U.S. naval forces in the Pacific prepared to seize California ports if war broke out.

Meanwhile, Mexican authorities in California had their hands full with events on shore. One incident involved a small expedition that crossed the Sierras and entered California in December, 1845. The expedition was led by a United States Army captain, John Charles Frémont. Supposedly, Frémont was simply exploring and surveying territories in the West, but the Mexicans were naturally suspicious.

Saying that he needed to buy supplies, Frémont spent some time in and near Monterey early in 1846. Then he and his men surprised the authorities by building a log fort atop Hawk's Peak, about 25 miles away. To the outrage of the Mexican officials, Frémont proceeded to raise an American flag over the fort!

Needless to say, Frémont's actions made him a very unpopular character with the local government. Fortunately for all concerned, the Americans soon abandoned their makeshift fort and headed north toward the Oregon Country.

Meanwhile, another American had set out on a secret mission to California. A lieutenant in the U.S. Marines, he crossed into Mexico disguised as a merchant. His real "business" was to deliver messages to California from American officials in Washington.

After making his way to Monterey, the secret agent picked up Frémont's trail and followed him to Oregon. Catching up with the expedition in May, he delivered the messages he had carried all the way from Washington.

To this day no one knows exactly what was in the messages. Possibly they contained orders to Frémont

from United States President James K. Polk. What *is* known is that Frémont abruptly turned around and headed back to California. There his name became linked with one of the most colorful episodes in California lore—the famed Bear Flag Revolt.

This brief episode involved a small band of settlers and leather-clad frontiersmen in the area of Sonoma, north of San Francisco Bay. By the middle of 1846, these Americans were worried that they might be thrown out of California. Perhaps encouraged by Frémont, in June they decided to stage a revolt.

Since they didn't officially represent the U.S. government, the Americans couldn't very well raise the Stars and Stripes and claim California for the United States. Instead, they designed a homemade flag on a piece of unbleached cotton. They chose a red star to stand for independence, and a brown grizzly bear to represent strength and courage. Under these symbols they printed the words "California Republic." At least as far as this ragtag group of rebels was concerned, the world had just gained a new country! (Many years later, their simple banner provided the basic design for the California state flag.)

Of course, Mexican authorities saw these activities as highly illegal. The Bear Flaggers engaged in a number of other unlawful acts as well. They stole horses and took people captive (including the respected Mexican general Mariano Guadalupe Vallejo). They also seized property. In fact, they made their headquarters in Vallejo's northern California stronghold of Sonoma. It was there that they raised their flag on June 14, 1846.

Even Americans were troubled by some of these actions, especially those who had lived in California for a long time. Many of them shared the Bear Flaggers' hope that California would separate from Mexico and eventually become part of the United States. But they didn't always approve of the way the rebels were trying to achieve their goal.

Interestingly, neither the Americans nor the Mexican authorities knew that events in other places were already making the rebellion seem like "small potatoes." A few months before, United States and Mexican forces had fought a brief skirmish along the Rio Grande, near the Texas-Mexico border. In May, the U.S. Congress agreed to President Polk's request and declared war. This news had not yet reached California. So, when the rebels began the Bear Flag Revolt, they didn't know that the United States and Mexico had already been at war for nearly a month!

While the Bear Flaggers made plans to add additional land to their Republic, an event of much more importance began to unfold in Monterey. With the *Californios* in the capital community looking on, a United States naval force was repeating Commodore Jones's "conquest" of 1842. But this time the conquest was no mistake.

Soon Frémont and his men were hurrying south to join the American force in Monterey. By July 9, the California Republic was no more. The Bear Flag had given way to the Stars and Stripes.

## A Change of Flags

When the Bear Flag revolt broke out, Commodore John Drake Sloat of the United States Navy was sailing at a fast clip to Monterey from the area of Mazatlán, Mexico. Like

Commodore Jones before him, Sloat was the commander of American naval forces in the Pacific. Also like Jones, he had orders to seize harbors on the California coast in the event of war with Mexico.

Sloat had received unofficial news that Americans and Mexicans were already fighting in Texas. He knew that a formal declaration of war might come any day. And like Commodore Jones in 1842, he had reason to think that the British might be headed for Monterey to claim this Pacific prize for England. So Sloat was sailing for California to occupy the port before the British could.

Sloat reached Monterey Bay on July 2, 1846. The commodore had sent two ships from the Pacific Squadron ahead of him, and he was glad to find them safely at anchor in the bay. He was also relieved that no British warships were anywhere to be seen.

Sloat knew very well that Americans had raised their flag over Monterey by mistake a few years earlier. Before taking any action, he tried to find out all he could about what was going on in California. He read official documents and met with the American consul, Thomas Oliver Larkin. He learned about the Bear Flag uprising to the north, including the capture of General Vallejo.

But one thing Sloat could not find out was whether war had been declared between the United States and Mexico. News of Congress's action in May had still not reached California.

After pondering all he had learned and consulting with the commanders of his other two ships, Sloat decided it was time to act. Early on the morning of July 7, he sent a message to shore demanding the surrender of Monterey.

About three hours later, a detachment of 250 U.S.
Marines and seamen headed for the bay town. Once on
shore, they marched straight to the Custom House (a
government building where non-Mexican shippers paid
special taxes called custom fees). There a proclamation
was read to the townspeople and Mexican officials in both
English and Spanish. The proclamation informed them
that "a state of war" existed with Mexico, and that
California now belonged to the United States!

With that, the Stars and Stripes were raised, and
each American ship in the harbor fired a 21-gun salute.
The United States had just laid claim to approximately
600,000 square miles of Mexican territory! Yet the local
officials did not attempt to resist Sloat and his men, in

part because California Governor Pio Pico was head-quartered far to the south, in Los Angeles. For the second time in less than four years, Monterey fell without a fight.

Eight days later, Sloat, who was in poor health, turned his command over to Commodore Robert Field Stockton. A man of action, Stockton moved quickly to raise the American flag over many of California's outlying settlements. To accomplish this, he reorganized John Charles Frémont's expedition and promoted Frémont to the rank of major.

The new major's force included both U.S. soldiers and a number of American settlers who volunteered their services. These men became known as the California Battalion of Mounted Riflemen (or, more simply, the California Battalion). With little opposition from the *Californios*, the battalion was soon hoisting the American flag over a number of settlements.

Stockton had already sent another officer to seize the harbor at Yerba Buena (soon to be known as San Francisco). Meanwhile, the commodore himself traveled south to Los Angeles and took control of the pueblo there.

Before returning to Monterey, Stockton named Archibald Gillespie as the man in charge of Los Angeles. Gillespie was the former secret agent and Marine lieutenant who had delivered the mysterious messages to Frémont in Oregon. Promoted to captain by Stockton, he was left in command of a small garrison of about 50 men.

After Commodore Stockton took his leave, Gillespie set about enforcing the rules Stockton had laid down (as well as some that he may have thought of himself). And that is when the trouble began that led to the heroics of Lean John.

# *Trouble in Los Angeles*

The Americans' new laws included some that seemed unrealistic and unfair to many of the townspeople in Los Angeles. For example, they were told that they could not be outside their homes after a certain hour of night, and that two or more people could not walk the streets together.

The *Angeleños* (residents of Los Angeles) were not used to being told how to act in their own town— especially by foreigners like these haughty Americans! Soon resentment toward the newcomers began to grow.

Gillespie's attitude toward the *Angeleños* didn't help matters. He showed little respect for the local people or their customs, and he threatened harsh punishments against those who disobeyed his commands. According to several sources, these threats were frequently carried out, with arrests being "freely made." As tensions continued to mount between the residents and the American force, talk of rebellion began to be heard in the pueblo.

Finally, some of the *Californios* decided to take matters into their own hands. The ringleaders are thought to have been a small group of ambitious Mexican officers. Gathering a band of about 500 horsemen, they surrounded the hill where Gillespie's men were quartered. The leaders of the revolt then turned the tables on the Americans by demanding that they surrender the garrison!

Gillespie knew that he was in desperate trouble. He and his men were outnumbered ten to one, and the garrison's supply of food and water would not last for long. Somehow, he had to get word of the trouble in Los

Angeles to Stockton's fighting force in Monterey. Meanwhile, he could try to hold out until help arrived.

But who could break through the *Californios'* lines to get a message to Stockton? The force surrounding the garrison was composed of some of the most expert horseback riders in the world. Besides, Stockton and his men were more than 300 miles away! Asking a messenger to outrace the *Californios* and deliver the message in time was like asking the impossible.

But the "impossible" was the only hope Captain Gillespie had.

# A Tall, Slender Swede

Among the 50 or so men that Gillespie had under his command was a lanky Swede (a person from the country of Sweden, in northern Europe). This was the man who was known as John Brown. Being tall and slender, he was also tagged with the nickname Juan Flaco, or "Lean John."

Brown was no stranger to adventure—or to fighting. Born in 1799 in far-off Sweden, he had left his homeland when he was about 15 years of age for an exciting and danger-filled life on the high seas.

Shortly after taking to the ocean, the young sailor got his first taste of war. At that time, several countries in Europe had banded together against the French military leader and emperor Napoleon Bonaparte. Although Brown was a Swedish sailor, he was serving under the flag of Great Britain. When Napoleon was finally defeated, Lean John was one of the seafarers who saw the famous emperor being taken to live in exile on the island of St. Helena (off the southwest coast of Africa).

After sailing the seas for a period of time, Brown found himself in South America. There he became involved in the wars being fought for independence from Spain. While fighting for the patriot leader Simon Bolívar (known as "The Liberator"), Lean John served in both the army and the navy. This "double duty" enabled him to cross the Isthmus of Panama four times, round Cape Horn (the tip of South America) at least three times, and fight in nine battles!

Eventually the fearless Swede was captured and sentenced to death. But Lean John's adventures were far

from over. Shortly before he was to be shot, he escaped on a Mexican vessel bound for California.

Arriving in southern California in 1828, Brown apparently found the place to his liking. He had learned English while serving with the British, and Spanish during his stay in South America. So the lanky Swede was able to fit in well with many of the people who lived in and around the small Mexican village of Los Angeles. To earn his keep, he did a number of different jobs, including trapping, clerking in a store, serving as an express rider, and working as a cowboy.

Brown also became involved in several fights over the way California was being governed. In the mid-1840s, he sided with Mexican Governor Manuel Micheltorena, who was trying to defend his government against a rival group. Among Lean John's allies in this dispute were a number of *Californios* and well-known foreign settlers, including John A. Sutter. (Sutter would become much more famous a few years later, when gold was discovered near Sutter's Mill.) Despite their help, Micheltorena was defeated and driven from office. Disappointed by this outcome, Lean John returned to Los Angeles.

After Micheltorena's defeat, Brown might have thought he was going to take a long siesta from fighting. If so, he was mistaken, for it was in the very next year (1846) that the United States seized control of California. Since he had been unhappy with the area's government, Lean John had little trouble deciding to side with the Americans. Joining the company commanded by Captain Gillespie, he helped to man the garrison atop the hill in Los Angeles.

And so it was that John Brown found himself part of the besieged force that the *Californios* had surrounded.

## The Only Man for the Job

Outmanned and outgunned, Captain Gillespie was desperate to find a man who was able and willing to make a run for Monterey. He knew that he needed a fearless and expert rider, and someone who knew the land.

Perhaps some of the men under Gillespie's command led him to the slender Swede who had recently joined the company. When he learned that the newcomer had all the qualifications—and could speak Spanish besides—Gillespie knew that he had found his man.

But would Lean John agree to go? Carefully, Gillespie outlined his plan and explained that it was the Americans' only hope. Leaving nothing to chance, he also offered Brown the handsome sum of $500 if he succeeded in getting a message to Commodore Stockton.

Upon hearing the captain out, Lean John pondered his offer. No one had to tell him that he would have only a slim chance of breaking through the *Californios'* lines. After that, he would have to ride day and night to reach Stockton in Monterey before the garrison fell. That would mean changing horses several times along the way, all the while eluding anyone who was in pursuit. And even if he succeeded in doing all of that, Stockton might still fail to reach Los Angeles in time to save the garrison and its men.

It sounded like an impossible task. Still, Lean John could see that the Americans had little choice. They had to try to get a messenger through, and he was the logical man for the job. Besides, he had been in many a tight scrape before. If he could cheat the executioner's squad in South America, maybe he could outwit and outrace the *Californios* too! To Gillespie's relief, he agreed to undertake the mission.

After being informed of the Swede's decision, the captain told him to pick the best horse and saddle from the company's supply. Upon careful inspection, Lean John selected a saddle that belonged to a lieutenant. But the horse he chose was his own. None of the others, he declared, were "in fit condition" for his use.

To keep the watchful *Californios* from guessing what was going on, the saddle was wrapped in a blanket before being carried to the place where Lean John's horse was kept. Then a special collection of handmade *cigaritos* (cigarettes or small cigars) was prepared. Before each cigarette was rolled, the paper was marked with Captain Gillespie's seal and the words "Believe the Bearer."

The idea was that Brown could give a marked cigarette to any "true American" he met, including Stockton himself. After seeing Gillespie's seal and reading the words on the paper, the Americans would know that the messenger could be trusted.

So that he could identify the special cigarettes, Brown put a black spot on the end of each one. Then he mixed them in with others he carried and stuffed them in his clothing. He even took the trouble to hide one or two of them in his long hair!

With the preparations completed, Lean John made the rounds saying goodbye to his friends. Neither he nor his companions knew whether they would see each other again.

By this time it was approaching eight o'clock in the evening. It was time for the brave Swede to strap on his spurs and begin the dangerous dash for help.

## A Mighty Leap

Hoisting himself into the saddle, Lean John murmured into the ear of his fleet white steed. After a quick check that all was ready, he asked a trooper to open the gate to the garrison and give the password to the sentinel stationed outside.

Unfortunately, upon opening the gate, the foolish trooper called out to the sentinel, telling him not to shoot the man on the white horse! Along with a commotion from a pack of barking dogs, the trooper's cry aroused the *Californios* who were camped nearby. Lean John spurred his horse into motion, but he had gone only a short way before 15 armed *vaqueros* (cowboys) were on his trail!

Riding wildly, Lean John headed toward the Cahuenga Pass. The determined Swede did have one trick up his sleeve. It was here that his knowledge of the land— and his decision to ride his own proven horse—helped him make his getaway.

Approximately two miles from the garrison, Brown approached a deep ravine. Thirteen feet wide, the gulch cut right through the trail he was following. Lean John knew that the only way across was to jump!

When his pursuers realized what he had in mind, they pulled out their guns and started shooting. The Swede and his mount were within a few feet of the ravine when one of the bullets found its mark. It struck

the galloping horse in the right flank, just behind Lean John's leg.

Perhaps the shock gave the animal an added boost, for it made a mighty leap. With its rider hanging on for dear life, the gallant steed cleared the gulch with only inches to spare!

Looking back over his shoulder, Lean John laughed to see his outraged pursuers stranded on the opposite side of the ravine. Try as they might, they couldn't get their horses to make the jump! Before long the vanquished *vaqueros* disappeared from sight. Bending forward in the saddle, Brown urged his mount on. He had made it through the *Californios'* lines, but his journey was only beginning.

## Lean John Makes a Friend

Lean John's relief did not last for long. Soon after jumping the ravine, his courageous steed began to falter. After about two miles the mighty horse collapsed and fell to the ground—dead!

Upon inspecting the fallen animal, Brown discovered the bullet wound in its flank. It was the first time that he realized that his mount had been shot.

Sadly, Lean John stripped off the saddle and hung it on the branch of a nearby tree. Pulling off his spurs, he gave a last look back at the brave white horse. Then he set off at a run for a friend's ranch—27 miles away!

All through the night Lean John hurried toward the ranch. By the time he reached his goal, dawn was about to break. He was so exhausted that he could barely stagger up to the door of the ranch house. When he aroused the

owner, Domingo Domínguez, his appearance shocked the sleepy rancher. Naturally, Domínguez demanded to know what had happened.

As tired as he was, Lean John was still thinking quickly. He didn't know how Domínguez might feel about the uprising in Los Angeles. Instead of confessing his real mission, he told the rancher that he had been chasing a thief when a grizzly bear came out of the bushes and frightened his horse.

This tale seemed to satisfy Domínguez, as grizzlies were known to frequent the area. Waking his wife, the rancher asked her to fix their exhausted guest a hearty breakfast. Meanwhile, he had a fresh mount rounded up.

Refreshed by the food and the horn of brandy he used to wash it down, Lean John soon was ready to resume his journey. But Domínguez had a surprise in store. Thinking that Brown was still in pursuit of a thief, his host insisted that he take a man named Tom Lewis with him for safety's sake. Lean John had little choice but to agree.

Shortly after daybreak, Brown and Lewis mounted their horses and waved farewell to the rancher. But when Lean John made a beeline for Santa Barbara after leaving the ranch—showing no sign of chasing a thief—his companion grew curious. Eventually Lewis questioned the slender Swede about the real purpose of his ride.

Knowing that Lewis was an American (he hailed from Boston, Massachusetts), Lean John figured that he could trust him to side with Gillespie and his men rather than the *Californios*. As they galloped along, he described what had taken place in Los Angeles and the message he was carrying to Stockton.

The Bostonian's reaction told Lean John that he had been right to share his secret. As the sun rose higher in the sky, Captain Gillespie's messenger felt his spirits rising, too. It was good to be on his way again, with a belly warmed by food and a fresh mount beneath him. And it didn't hurt at all that now he had a new friend at his side.

## *Followed!*

Around 11 o'clock that night, Brown and Lewis rode wearily into the town of Santa Barbara. Since escaping from Los Angeles the night before, the lanky Swede had traveled more than 75 miles. This was a remarkable feat, considering that he had covered about a third of the distance on foot!

Upon arriving in Santa Barbara, the dust-covered riders were anxious to head for the small American garrison commanded by Captain Theodore Talbot.

However, at that late hour they were unable to gain entrance into the military barracks. Forced to wait until dawn, they used the time for some much-needed rest.

The next morning, the two men were taken to see the garrison's commander. After giving Talbot one of Gillespie's marked cigarettes, Brown told him about the revolt at Los Angeles. The concerned captain immediately began giving orders to prepare for a possible uprising in Santa Barbara. Meanwhile, he had his men gather suitable animals for Lean John and his companion.

Equipped by Captain Talbot with new mounts as well as extra horses, Brown and Lewis resumed their race up the California coast. Riding like the wind, they guided the horses toward Stockton's Monterey headquarters. When the animals they were riding grew tired of carrying their weight, they quickly dismounted and threw their saddles on the spares. In this way they were able to keep riding hard until they reached the ranch of an American and former ship captain, Thomas M. Robbins.

When they arrived at the Robbins homestead, Lean John pulled out another of his special cigarettes. The rancher listened intently as the thin Swede described his mission. Upon seeing the mark of Gillespie's ring, Robbins was eager to help. Quickly he rustled up a welcome breakfast for the hungry travelers. After supplying them with new saddles and four fresh horses, he wished them luck and sent them on their way.

Shortly after leaving the ranch, Brown and Lewis looked back upon it from a nearby mountain. It was then that they realized they were being followed! About two dozen riders were heading their way, bearing lances that glistened in the sun. Even though the *Californios*

hesitated at the base of the mountain and seemed to turn back, Lean John had little doubt who they were looking for.

Brown and Lewis were not about to wait around to see whether the lancers picked up their trail. Urging their mounts on, they crossed the mountain and continued on their way as fast as the horses would carry them.

It wasn't until later that Lean John learned what happened to his latest pursuers. As it turned out, the lancers had arrived at the Robbins ranch shortly after Brown and Lewis departed. When they inquired whether the rancher had seen "Juan Flaco," Robbins told them that he had recently passed through and taken four of his best animals. Upon hearing this news, the *Californios* demanded fresh horses for themselves.

Apparently eager to cooperate, the rancher called for

his cowboys. Quietly, he told them to round up the worst animals they could find! Showing the broken-down beasts to the lancers, Robbins announced that they were the best he had to offer. He added that his visitors were welcome to take their pick.

The disgusted *Californios* refused this offer and decided to continue north on their own weary mounts. Robbins's quick thinking had prevented them from obtaining fresh horses, giving Brown and Lewis precious time to put space between themselves and their pursuers!

Safe from the lancers, the two "express riders" made their next stop at a ranch owned by a man from Tennessee, Lewis T. Burton. Arriving at the ranch house late in the evening, Lean John handed the owner one of Gillespie's cigarettes. After inspecting it, Burton listened to the messenger's account. Then this "true American" (as Lean John later described him) rounded up four of his best horses to lend to the weary travelers.

Leaving Robbins's played-out animals behind, Lean John asked Burton to return them to their owner if he could. As for the Tennesseean's own horses, Brown told him to look for them in Monterey. With that, the two gallant horsemen once again hit the trail.

Somewhere between the mission towns of San Luis Obispo and San Miguel, Brown and Lewis stopped to make camp and grab a little shuteye. Awakening a few hours later, a groggy Lean John found his companion too sick from fatigue to mount up. Knowing that only rest could cure his ills, the Swede left Lewis $20 and the two animals they had ridden during the night. He then told him that he must care for himself and not tell anyone that they had been together.

After a final handshake, Lean John climbed into the saddle. Waving a farewell salute to his exhausted friend, he lit out for Monterey and his long-awaited meeting with Stockton.

## *The Last Lap*

Saddle-sore and bone-weary, Lean John rode into the capital community, anxious to meet Stockton and complete his mission. But heartbreaking news awaited him. Commodore Stockton had recently sailed for San Francisco!

Lean John was crushed. He had come so far and survived so many dangers, and now he was unable to deliver his message to the only man who could make a difference!

The Montereyans who heard Brown's story were concerned by the tale of trouble in Los Angeles. Thanking the exhausted messenger for his courageous ride, they tried to give him some supper. But Lean John was too fatigued to eat. Gladly accepting the offer of a place to rest, he flung himself on the bed and soon was fast asleep.

While Brown slept, a group of local leaders met to discuss what to do. (One of them was the respected American alcalde, or mayor, of Monterey, Walter Colton.) All agreed that Gillespie's message had to be delivered to Stockton in San Francisco. But who could be trusted to get it there?

It didn't take long for the Montereyans to decide that there was only one person who could finish the job—Lean John himself! The trip might be dangerous, for the whole area might erupt when news of the revolt in southern

California spread. The brave Swede had already shown that he could handle whatever came his way. Besides, Stockton would want to hear firsthand about the situation in Los Angeles.

With their minds made up, the group roused Lean John from his slumber after only a half-hour of rest. Expecting that he would be reluctant to resume his journey, they offered him an additional $200 to deliver Gillespie's message personally to Stockton in San Francisco.

After a moment's thought, Brown consented to complete the last lap of his trip. But there was one condition—he must be given an extra-fast horse to start out on. The Montereyans agreed and set about making the arrangements. Meanwhile, Lean John promptly went back to sleep.

After about three hours, he was awakened again. Stiff from the pounding his body had taken, the slender Swede could barely get out of bed. Requesting a bowl of cold water, he washed himself as best he could. Then he dressed quickly and gulped down some coffee.

Feeling somewhat refreshed, Brown went outside to eye the horse that had been provided for him. After a quick inspection he pronounced himself satisfied. The mount was, indeed, a fast one, as it was a race horse owned by an American named Job Dye. With a letter of introduction supplied by the Montereyans, Lean John set off for San Francisco.

Most of the townspeople were still asleep as Dye's horse pounded around the curving shoreline of Monterey Bay. Before long it had carried its rider to the ranch of

Anjel Castro. Patting the heaving sides of the race horse, Brown stiffly dismounted and headed for the ranch house.

After seeing the letter Lean John had brought from Monterey, Castro set to work rounding up a relay of animals. About an hour later Brown was again making tracks.

His next stop was at a ranch owned by Antonio German. He showed German his letter and waited a little more than an hour while fresh horses were obtained and made ready. Once more heading north, he made a third stop for another change of animals before reaching the town of San Jose.

When he arrived in San Jose, Lean John immediately looked for Captain C. M. Weber, who could provide him with additional horses. Unfortunately, the captain was in San Francisco! Frustrated, the anxious messenger tried to find someone else who could lend him some fresh animals.

It was at this point that Lean John had a chance meeting with Thomas O. Larkin. This influential American was a resident of Monterey. Among other honors, he was the first United States consul in Mexican California. (You may remember that Commodore Sloat met with Larkin before seizing the capital.)

After seeing one of Gillespie's cigarettes, and learning of the events in Los Angeles, Larkin immediately obtained more horses. But the delay in San Jose had been costly. All together, Lean John had lost about four hours. When he finally climbed back into the saddle, he set off at a gallop. To quote from his own account, he passed Santa Clara "fluking"!

Night had fallen by the time Brown finally pulled up on the shore of San Francisco Bay. As he looked across the water at Stockton's ship (the U.S. frigate *Congress*), he heard the boom of the eight o'clock gun announcing the hour. Lean John cursed the time he had lost in San Jose. He had arrived too late to see the commodore that night. There was nothing to do but stretch out on the beach and wait for morning.

## *Stockton at Last*

When daybreak came, Lean John hailed the market boat from the *Congress*. Upon hearing the importance of his message, the boat's crew immediately agreed to row him out to the ship.

Once aboard the frigate, the bone-weary messenger was taken to Commodore Stockton's quarters. Face to face with the American commander at last, Brown gave him the last of Gillespie's cigarettes and described the

situation in Los Angeles. Between sips of brandy, he told the commodore that there was no time to lose if the garrison was to be saved.

Gravely, Stockton thanked the tall Swede who had come so far to deliver Gillespie's plea for help. Lean John nodded and took his leave. He had done his duty. The rest was up to Stockton.

History tells us that the American commodore wasted little time in acting upon Gillespie's message. At once he ordered a relief ship to be prepared. Loaded with supplies and reinforcements, the ship departed San Francisco Bay for the port of San Pedro (near Los Angeles). Aboard the ship, according to some reports, was none other than Lean John, returning south with the reinforcements.

Back in Los Angeles, the surrounded Americans were trying to hold out until help arrived. Of course, Captain Gillespie had no way of knowing whether his message had reached Stockton. For all he knew, Lean John had been captured, injured, or even killed. Meanwhile, the *Californios* were offering generous terms of surrender. With no relief in sight, Gillespie felt he had no choice but to accept the offer.

So, with flags flying and drums beating, the small American force abandoned the garrison and marched out of Los Angeles. Under the terms of the surrender, they were able to take their weapons with them. But they were to go directly to the port of San Pedro, and from there leave southern California by sea.

Upon reaching San Pedro, Gillespie succeeded in stalling for time. This action proved crucial, for Stockton's reinforcements soon arrived. Once the two groups of

Americans joined forces, the terms of the truce with the *Californios* were quickly forgotten. The Americans immediately began making plans to try to recapture Los Angeles.

## The Second Taking of California

The fight that followed is often called the Battle of the Old Woman's Gun. According to most sources, the gun in question was an antique four-pound cannon that had once been on display in the town plaza. Reportedly, an old woman hid the cannon in her garden when the Americans first took control of the town, so that they would not be able to use it. When Gillespie's men were driven out of the settlement, the gun was hauled out and mounted on a pair of wagon wheels. The *Californios* then took it to the site of the battle (the Domínguez Rancho). There it proved its worth by helping them defeat the combined U.S. forces.

While the *Californios* celebrated their victory, the Americans retreated to San Pedro, carrying their dead and wounded with them. Up to six of their men had lost their lives in the fight to retake Los Angeles. Before taking their leave, the Americans buried the dead on a small island near the San Pedro shore. To this day the island is known as Dead Man's Island.

With the burials accomplished, the survivors sailed to San Diego. There they were joined by Commodore Stockton and additional reinforcements.

While these events were taking place, the rebellion spread across the countryside. Soon much of the land between San Diego and Santa Barbara was once again in the hands of the *Californios*.

This set the stage for several skirmishes and pitched battles. The individual acts of heroism during this time may have even included a second remarkable feat by Lean John. According to legend, he was *again* called upon to carry a message through enemy lines!

As the fighting continued, more Americans joined the scene. They included troops brought from the area of present-day New Mexico. These men were under the command of General Stephen Watts Kearny of the U.S. Army. Exhausted and poorly fed, Kearny's men arrived just in time to face the *Californios* in the Battle of San Pasqual (northeast of San Diego) on December 6, 1846.

This fierce fight pitted the saber-wielding Americans against determined *Californios* armed with lances. By the time it was over, 21 of Kearny's men lay dead, and many more were wounded. Only about a dozen of their foes suffered wounds. Afterwards the surviving Americans

retreated to a hilltop. During the next few days they had to eat their mules in order to keep from starving to death.

The Battle of San Pasqual was the high point of the *Californios'* brave attempt to regain control of their land. After Kearny's men joined with Commodore Stockton's forces in San Diego, the tide began to turn.

On January 10, 1847, the Americans recaptured Los Angeles. Three days later, the *Californios* officially ended their struggle. The surrender was accepted at Cahuenga by none other than our old friend John Charles Frémont (of Hawk's Peak fame).

This second taking of California was much bloodier than the first. The *Californios* proved to be valiant warriors, and many lives were lost before the last shot was fired. But when the dust settled, it was once again the Stars and Stripes that flew over Alta California.

Although peace reigned in California, the war between Mexico and the United States continued for some time. The conflict was finally settled by the Treaty of Guadalupe Hidalgo in February, 1848.

As part of this historic agreement, the Mexican government officially yielded a huge amount of land to the United States. This vast area included the present-day states of California, Nevada, Utah, and New Mexico, as well as parts of Arizona, Colorado, Kansas, and Wyoming. In return, the U.S. government agreed to pay Mexico more than $15 million.

This outcome made many people wonder why the war had been fought in the first place. After all, the United States had tried to buy the same territory from Mexico a few years before! In addition, many Americans thought they had just purchased a wasteland filled with barren mountains and empty deserts. One well-known Army officer even said that he would not trade two eastern counties for all of the Far West!

But no one could foresee that the land given up by Mexico was—literally—a gold mine. Just as the war was being settled, an event occurred that changed the history of California forever. Among other things, this event brought men rushing to the area from around the world and speeded up California's entry into the Union as the 31st state.

Today, such an event would be instant news. But as I

said earlier, in those days it took time for information to travel from place to place. And so it was that Mexico officially gave up its claim to California in a treaty signed on February 2, 1848—nine days *after* James W. Marshall found gold at Sutter's Mill!

## California's Horseback Hero

In closing this book, I would like to return to the question I asked at the beginning. Was Lean John truly a hero?

To begin with, there is little doubt that the slender Swede's ride was an amazing display of courage, endurance, and horsemanship. Although there is some question about exactly how far he traveled, and how long his journey took, few people in history have even attempted such a feat.

Several estimates have been given of the number of miles Lean John covered. In his own account (written in 1858), he gave the distance as 630 miles. Captain Gillespie's narrative (also written in 1858) put the figure closer to 600. A similar estimate was made by Monterey alcalde Walter Colton (in a book published soon after the event, in 1850).

Other estimates have been as low as 450 miles. Interestingly, today's mileage charts give approximately this figure as the distance between Los Angeles and San Francisco (by way of Monterey). Of course, what these charts show is *highway* miles. It's safe to say that Lean John covered much more ground than that. All things considered, I believe we should probably credit him with traveling somewhere around 600 miles. And let's not forget that he *ran* about 27 of those miles himself!

We should also remember that Brown's ride was not always over clear-cut trails and smooth paths (never mind highways!). Instead, his route took him over wooded hillsides, brush-covered flatlands, and coastal mountains. He had to cross hazardous valleys and rocky canyons, and deal with such things as steep cliffs, deep ravines, treacherous rivers, and confusing cross-trails. And all the while the lanky messenger had to be constantly on the lookout for familiar faces and fresh mounts—not to mention hostile *Californios!*

How long did his dangerous trek take him? Again, estimates vary. Lean John himself said that he completed the trip in four days—and you'd think he would know! Still, others have suggested that it took him either slightly more or slightly less time. Either way, for much of that time, he was jolting in the saddle both day and night in his quest to get Gillespie's message to Commodore Stockton. And he made do with less rest and food than most people who just work at a desk all day!

As remarkable as Lean John's ride was, it might be said that he failed to achieve his purpose. As I have described, the garrison surrendered before Stockton's reinforcements could arrive. In addition—and sad to tell—the lanky Swede never received a penny of the money he was promised!

Nor did lasting fame come to John Brown. Today his remains lie in an unmarked grave in a bustling valley town located in the heart of California. Strange to say, the site of his final resting place is none other than the city of

Stockton—a place named after the very man Lean John rode so long and so hard to see.

So, was Lean John a hero? I'll let you decide. But there's one last fact I'd like you to consider, and it is perhaps the most amazing of all. At the time of his grueling ride, this "California cowboy" from a far-off land was 47 years old!

# *Author's Notes*

An important part of each book in the **History & Happenings of California Series** is the Author's Notes section. It is here that additional information is presented so that readers can better appreciate the **events, people,** and **places** discussed in the text.

Lean John's ride, and the other events described in this book, are historical fact. However, it is important to note that various sources disagree about certain details. This is not surprising to most people who write about the past, as they know that history is not cut-and-dried. Both in the text itself and in these Notes I indicate some of the bits of information that are subject to some dispute. (An example is the discussion, near the end of the story, of exactly how far Lean John rode, and how long his ride took him.)

As I noted in the Introduction, there have been many other horseback heros in American history. For those who wish to pursue the stories of **Paul Revere** and **Sybil Ludington,** information about their lives and deeds can be found in most public libraries. Certainly, **Henry Wadsworth Longfellow's** poem "Paul Revere's Ride" is worth looking up. However, keep in mind that Longfellow wrote this work more than 80 years after the events that it describes. Historians have pointed out that he took a few liberties with the facts in creating his poem.

A little research will also uncover a number of tales about the exploits of riders for the famed **Pony Express.** The story of the "pony boys" is an exciting, if brief, chapter in United States history. With all the dangers the express riders faced, it's hard to believe that in over 650,000 miles of riding, only one messenger was killed in the line of duty. Perhaps most amazing of all, only once was the mail lost!

In my opinion, however, it would be hard to find a horseback feat to rival the one described in this book. Before discussing it further, I would like to make a few comments about the historical background provided in the text.

Upon reading about the mistaken "conquest" of Monterey by **Commodore Thomas ap Catesby Jones,** some may wonder (as I did) what the "ap" in his name stands for. After a little checking, I was surprised to learn that it is a Welsh word meaning "son of."

As discussed in the text, trouble between the United States and Mexico was the underlying cause of many of the events leading up to Lean John's ride. Since the United States won the war, and greatly expanded its territory as a result, Americans tend to forget that the war wasn't popular with everyone at the time. Bitter debates raged in Congress and around the country over the conflict. A number of U.S. citizens and leaders believed that it was wrong to try to seize Mexican territory by force. One well-known politician who criticized the war (after supporting it for a time) was future president Abraham Lincoln.

Speaking of would-be presidents, one of the characters in our tale was later nominated for president himself. In fact, **John Charles Frémont** was the first Republican candidate for president, in 1856. (Lincoln was the second, in 1860.)

Of course, few could have foreseen Army captain Frémont's future fame at the time of the **Hawk's Peak** incident. Although this temporary raising of an American flag over a log fort was a relatively minor event, some historians describe it as "the first open act of hostility" in the American conquest of California. Incidentally, more than one source indicates that the flag in question was a banner of the U.S. Army Corps of Engineers, rather than the Stars and Stripes. Those who wish to learn more about this episode should know that Hawk's Peak is also known as Fremont Peak and as Gabilan (Gavilan) Peak. It is located near the historic mission town of San Juan Bautista.

I should mention that various accounts give quite different descriptions of the makeup and purpose of Frémont's expedition to California and other parts of the West. However, most sources do agree that his band included scouts (Kit Carson and Joseph Walker being among the best known), topographers (map makers and those who recorded land features), soldiers (probably around 60), and up to six Delaware Indians (who are thought to have acted as Frémont's bodyguards). Also a part of the expedition were a number of African Americans who had freed themselves from slavery.

As California history buffs know, both John Charles Frémont and his wife, Jessie, led colorful lives. Jessie became a talented and respected writer, while John Charles served as the American governor of California under military rule (for a 50-day span in 1847). In 1850 Frémont became one of California's first United States senators. As I mentioned earlier, six years later he was nominated for president. Unfortunately, he also suffered some serious setbacks. After several years of near poverty he is reported to have died alone in 1890, in a New York City boarding house.

The **Bear Flag Revolt** was, like the Hawk's Peak incident, a somewhat minor affair, considering that it was confined to a small area north of San Francisco and involved only a relative handful of rebels. However, as I noted in the text, this episode did give California the basic design for its state flag, which was officially adopted in 1911.

The short-lived California Republic established by the Bear Flaggers was abandoned with Commodore John Drake Sloat's seizure of the port of Monterey. In describing this event, I mention that the capital community's **Custom House** was a government building that was used to collect fees from foreign shipping. Interestingly, it is at the Custom House that Lean John is thought to have rested when he reached Monterey during his pursuit of Stockton.

This aged structure is still very much a part of the Monterey scene. Often described as the oldest public building on the Pacific coast, the Custom House also boasts the honor of being California's first Registered State Historical Landmark. Today it is part of the Monterey State Historic Park, and has been restored to look much as it did during its days as a working custom house. Located across from the entrance to Monterey's famed Fisherman's Wharf, the building is open to the public.

Commodore Sloat's successor, **Robert Field Stockton,** is another colorful figure. Like Lean John himself, Stockton saw action in many parts of the world. He began his naval career in 1811 and served in the War of 1812 against the British. He went on to see duty in the area of Africa, serving in the Algerian War and helping in the settlement of Liberia.

As commander of the *Congress,* it was Stockton who delivered the papers to Texas officially annexing the region to the United States. From there he continued to California, where he relieved Commodore Sloat.

By the way, Stockton went on to become the second military governor of California (from July 29, 1846, to January 19, 1847), and it was he who named Frémont as his successor. Like Frémont, the former commodore later served in the United States Senate (1851–1853), representing his native state of New Jersey.

Of course, it was also Stockton who left Archibald Gillespie in charge of the pueblo at **Los Angeles.** For those who are curious, I should note that the location of the hill where Gillespie and his men were supposedly quartered is something of a mystery—at least to me! Most sources don't even hint at the exact location. Considering all the changes in the Los Angeles area since that time, it seems safe to say that the hill was built upon, or perhaps even bulldozed down, long ago.

Several sources do indicate that the site of the American outpost was a place referred to as Fort Hill. If I lived in Los Angeles, I think it would be fun to obtain some old maps and try to figure out where Fort Hill was. Who knows, maybe a historical group could even be persuaded to put a plaque where Lean John began his remarkable ride!

As a hint to those who might want to seek out the site, let me say that one respected source states that the hilltop was "in the middle of Los Angeles." (Your job is to find out where the "middle" of Los Angeles was in 1846 . . . and where that would be today!) A second source (written more than a half century ago) suggests that Fort Hill was located atop a North Broadway hill that had a streetcar tunnel running through it. A third source indicates that the Church of Our Lady of the Angels is located on Fort Hill. (Is there such a church on North Broadway? Is it on a hill?) To confuse things even more, some say there may have been *two* Fort Hills in Los Angeles in the 1840s!

Finally, it's possible that Gillespie's garrison wasn't quartered on a hill at all. One credible source indicates that his small force "took refuge in the Government House." When this document was written (in 1937), the Government House site was occupied by the St. Charles Hotel, on Main Street in downtown Los Angeles.

It certainly would be nice to know where, exactly, Lean John began his daring journey. There are some other mysteries connected with **John Brown (Juan Flaco)** as well. One of them is the location of his original home in Sweden. According to an account of his death that appeared in the Sacramento *Daily Union* on December 14, 1859, he was born in the community, or area, of Carlescrona (Karlskrona). The exact date of his birth is also somewhat in doubt, as both the years 1799 and 1800 have been listed.

More important for our purposes are the facts of **Lean John's ride.** I have attempted to be accurate in describing his daring dash for help, using Brown's own account when possible. Once again, however, the details are often given differently in various sources, and it is impossible to be certain about every fact.

With this in mind I would like to mention that there are a number of published anecdotes and details that I chose to omit from my account. Although they are certainly colorful, many of them are questionable (to say the least). For example, I find it difficult to believe that as he was attempting to escape on foot (his horse having been shot), Lean John lashed out with a 60-foot lariat and wrapped it around the throat of one of his pursuers! I also question whether he then took his trusty Bowie knife and killed the unfortunate *Californio*. (Certainly nothing like this is mentioned in Brown's own account.)

It's also doubtful that Lean John fought many grizzly bears on his way north. For what it's worth, I'm not even sure that his clothes were made of tight-fitting buckskin, and I tend to picture him in boots rather than beaded doeskin mocassins. And while his blonde hair might have been long, I wonder whether it really hung to his shoulders.

Of course, different people can come to different con-clusions based on evidence that will never be perfect. I encourage those who have become intrigued by the tale of Lean John to do additional research on their own, and decide for themselves which information rings true.

Certainly the facts that are reasonably well established are exciting enough by themselves! For instance, how many of our nation's other horseback heros were pushing 50 years old when they made their trip? How many of their journeys lasted four to five days and covered up to 600 miles? How many of them had their horses shot out from under them and had to run a marathon to obtain another mount? (A marathon, by the way, is 26 miles, 385 yards. Lean John is thought to have run about 27 miles—over very uneven ground—to get to the Domínguez Rancho.)

In connection with this almost unbelievable race against time in the dead of night, it's of interest to note that—if we can believe the sources—Lean John *ran* considerably farther than Paul Revere rode!

Despite Brown's courage and endurance, not to mention his skill in horsemanship, his ride is not as well known today as many people think it should be. However, it would be unfair to leave the impression that it has been completely forgotten. Not only has Lean John's trip supposedly been mentioned in both poem and song, but during World War II a Liberty Ship was christened in his name. With the Stars and Stripes flying, the *Juan Flaco* proudly sailed the seas, a fitting tribute to the man who began his adult life as a sailor and ended his own narrative with the words "Juan Brown, a native of Sweden and a true American."

Fans of Lean John will be glad to know that he has been remembered more recently as well. In 1969, a historical marker honoring the slender Swede and his ride was placed at the corner of Weber and Union streets in the city of Stockton, near the former Citizen's Cemetery where "Juan Brown" was originally buried. I can only hope that this marker (California Registered Historical Landmark No. 513) will remind future generations of the marvelous exploits of California's own horseback hero.

# About the Author

Randall A. Reinstedt was born and raised on California's beautiful and historic Monterey Peninsula. After traveling widely throughout the world, he spent fifteen years teaching elementary school students, with special emphasis on California and local history. Today he continues to share his love of California's beauty and lore with young and old alike through his immensely popular publications. Among his many books is **More Than Memories: History & Happenings of the Monterey Peninsula,** an acclaimed history text for fourth-graders that is used in schools throughout the Monterey area.

Randy lives with his wife, Debbie, in a house overlooking the Pacific Ocean. In addition to his writing projects, he is in great demand as a lecturer on regional history to school and adult groups, and he frequently gives workshops for teachers on making history come alive in the classroom.

# About the Illustrator

A native Californian, Ed Greco has spent most of his professional career as a graphic designer and illustrator. Born and raised in the Santa Clara Valley, Ed grew up studying and illustrating northern California, its environment, and its history.

# Randall A. Reinstedt's
## History & Happenings of California Series

Through colorful tales drawn from the rich store of California lore, this series introduces young readers to the historical heritage of California and the West. "Author's Notes" at the end of each volume provide information about the people, places, and events encountered in the text. Whether read for enjoyment or for learning, the books in this series bring the drama and adventure of yesterday to the young people of today.

*Currently available in both hardcover and softcover:*

**Lean John, California's Horseback Hero**

**One-Eyed Charley, the California Whip**

**Otters, Octopuses, and Odd Creatures of the Deep**

**Stagecoach Santa**

**The Strange Case of the Ghosts of the Robert Louis Stevenson House**

**Tales and Treasures of California's Missions**

**Tales and Treasures of California's Ranchos**

**Tales and Treasures of the California Gold Rush**

**Hands-On History** teacher resource books are available to accompany titles in the **History & Happenings of California Series.** Packed with projects and activities integrating skills across the curriculum, these imaginative resource books help bring California history to life in the classroom.

*For information about the **History & Happenings of California Series,** as well as other titles by Randy Reinstedt for both children and adults, please write:*

GHOST TOWN PUBLICATIONS
P.O. Drawer 5998
Carmel, CA 93921